Abstracts of the

OBITUARY BOOK

1826 - 1849

Sussex County, Delaware

V. L. Skinner, Jr.

CLEARFIELD

Printed for Clearfield Company by
Genealogical Publishing Company
Baltimore, Maryland
2014

ISBN 978-0-8063-5707-2

Introduction

Sussex Co. is the southern most county of Delaware. Initially part of Pennsylvania, and partly claimed by Maryland, Sussex Co. has records dating from 1680. Many of the families of Sussex Co. can trace their roots back to Maryland's Eastern Shore and to Virginia's Eastern Shore.

The original of these abstracts was found in Lewes DE in 1954. Most of the names listed were residents of Sussex Co. The original was presented to the Daughters of the American Revolution, Washington, D.C. Library by the Col. David Hall Chapter in December 1954.

Included in this book of obituaries are names of the deceased, date of death, and often their age.

Abbreviations

c/o	child of
d/o	daughter of
s/o	son of

p. 1 ...		**Age**
20 July 1820	William Clark	65
	1826	
7 February	Thomas Simpler	8
10 February	Leah Simpler	<n/g>
23 February	Jesse Johnson	28
22 February	Winny Joseph wife of Ephraim	23
18 February	Samuel H. Carey	42
	Hester Prettyman wife of George	30
10 February	Elizabeth Joseph wife of Samuel	39
17 February	Margaret Wilson widow of William	88
22 February	William Holstein	30
4 March	Elisha Cohoon – 1 & 2 a.m.	31
8 or 9 March	James Hall	34
	William Stephenson	34
	Ann Fannell	17
26 March	Richard A. Dutten	22
8 April	Eleanor Walls wife of Samuel	50
18 April	John Sharp	52
p. 2 ...		
22 April	David Marvil	30
1 May	Benjamin Warren	36
16 May	Mitchell Scott, Jr.	29
	Lydia Walls wife of Solomon	26
20 May	Elizabeth Gordon wife of William	40
19 May	(N) Steel wife of James	<n/g>
27 June	Sophia Ennis wife of William	30
5 June	Nancy Stokely widow of Benjamin	25

2 June	Metilda Lewis	22
5 June	Elizabeth Lacey widow of Spencer	45
6 June	William B. Ennis	58
17 July	Burton Pepper	36
20 July	Abram Johnson	21
25 July	Comfort Mariner wife of Robert	40
29 July	Ruth Steel wife of Benjamin	45
30 July	Patience Willson of Richard	11
p. 3 ...		
13 August	Tabitha Morris widow of Lacey	<n/g>
19 August	Angelia (Hannah) Dodd, Sr.	70
24 August	Lodowick Conaway, Jr.	20
18 or 19 September	James Brown husband of Elizabeth	<n/g>
24 September	Mary Blue wife of Joel	30
25 September	Joseph Bennum	33
26 September	William McIlvaine	47
28 September	Nancy Godwin wife of Joseph	35
21 September	Straton Burton	32
29 September	Robert Lacey, Sr.	73
30 September	Zadoc James	69
29 September	(N) c/o Peter Rust	<n/g>
2 November	(N) c/o Newbould Coffin	<n/g>
	James Carpenter	<n/g>
2 or 3 November	James Tharp	<n/g>
26 to 30 December	James Middleton – murdered	30
p. 4 ...		

1827		
5 January	Priscilla Warren wife of Asa	30
7 January	Peter c/o Lemuel Johnson	31 days
8 January	Elon Joseph of Elisha – died by fire	14
18 January	Capt. Eli Carey	40
3 March	Selick Hazzard	50
15 March	James West, Jr.	23
	Tindley Bevans	26
26 March	John Messick	<n/g>
30 March	Rev. John Collins – 5 o'clock p.m.	50
	Elizabeth Marvel	<n/g>
6 April	Patience Clifton wife of Isaih	45
14 April	George Wise	36
17-18 July	Alice Lingo wife of Henry, Sr.	70
28 July	John Lingo, Sr.	58
26 July	Capt. David Parker	23
31 July	Charles Vaughn, Sr.	65
p. 5 ...		
5 August	Anna Carey wife of Thomas	30
	Rhoda Ellis	<n/g>
25 August	(N) c/o Henry Lawson	1 day
9 October	Ann M. Joseph wife of Paynter	22
21 October	Samuel P. Johnson of Richard	4
24 November	(N) c/o Elzey Palmore	few months
8 December	Lodawick Wilson – found dead	33
9 December	Robinson C. Waples	36
1828		

26 January	Thomas Wilson Carpenter	45
29 January	Zechariah Heaitt	68
30 January	William Quigg (collier)	40
1 February	Elizabeth Coulter (widow)	72
11 February	Job Pool – 1 o'clock p.m.	30
25 or 26 February	Samuel Dickinson	45
26-28 February	Woolsey Waples	<n/g>
29 February	Robert Warren – clerk	19
p. 6 ...		
29 February	Mary Campbell wife of (N)	25
6 April	Charles M. Cullen	60
	Pemberton Burton	28
5 April	Isaac Holland of (N)	<n/g>
7 April	Sarah Johnson wife of William, Sr. – 11 o'clock	64
15 April	Nathaniel Lawson – 2 o'clock	32
27 April	Jessee Dean, Jr.	24
28 April	Love Johnson widow of Slater	58
3 May	Lydia Prettyman wife of Burton – 11 o'clock	38
7 May	Mary B. Walls of James – by a fall	7
20 May	Priscilla L. Waples wife of Gideon – 10 o'clock	26
31 May	(N) c/o Henry Lawson	14 hours
29 May	Solomon Palmore	56
22 June	Mary Walls widow of Thomas, Sr.	71
5 July	Jessee Dean, Sr.	70

30 July	Samuel Burton of Samuel – fell from a horse	22
p. 7 ...		
29 July	Eliza White widow of Jacob	52
22 August	Burton Johnson – 5 o'clock; drowned	56
28 August	Elizabeth Blizzard wife of William – noon	26
1 September	Hannah Walls of Samuel – consumption	30
7 September	Jacob Jefferson, Jr. – 1 o'clock p.m.	19
10 September	John Davidson, Sr.	61
30 September	John Robertson (printer) – Dover	<n/g>
9 October	Thomas Collins - discutery	56
12 October	Henry W. Walls of John (carpenter)	3½ months
7 October	Benjamin L. Holland - pleurisy	34
4 December	Alice Watson	<n/g>
5 December	Nancy Morris wife of William of Ep.	24
	Nancy White wife of William	<n/g>
1829		
1 January	Joseph Tam	33
	Curtis Fisher	45
4 January	Prudence Hardy wife of John	40
p. 8 ...		
10 or 11 January	Jonathan Cullen	44
11 January	John Chase – 4 o'clock	60
15 January	Brinkley Ewing – old age	80
21 January	(N) c/o W. W. Johnson – a.m.	3 months 4 days

7 February	David McIlvaine – 2¼ a.m.	80
	Thomas Coleman (Lewis)	50
14 February	Martha Justis (widow)	60
19 February	Dr. Paul Waples	27
4 March	Joseph Holland	<n/g>
12-13 March	William H. Wells, Esq.	60
28 March	Ruth Palmore – colic	50
30 March	Nehemiah Hill	60
19 April	Rachel Morris wife of Wingate Morris	21
22 April	Mills Johnson – by a fall from a horse	4
9 May	Rachel Prettyman wife of William, & child	28
10 May	Martha Cannon – in jail	50
p. 9 ...		
15 May	James Lawson	65
7 June	Mary Blizzard	<n/g>
	James Hazzard	<n/g>
19 May	Nehemiah Maull (carpenter)	50
6 June	(N) c/o Thomas Coffin	<n/g>
8 June	(N) c/o Samuel Martin	<n/g>
12 June	(N) c/o Solomon Walls	4 or 5
18 July	Jonathan Dickison – drowned	21
26 July	Charles Dickeson – horse threw & fell on him	<n/g>
4 August	Nathan Palmore – by lightning & 4 oxen with him	17
7 August	James West, Sr.	58
14 August	Mary PettyJohn wife of Ebenezar	65
28 August	Martha Wilson wife of Joseph	60

1 September	Dr. John White (Lewes)	50
4 September	Jonathan Walls – thrown by a horse 3 days before	26
5 September	(N) c/o Kendal B. Atkins	3 weeks
p. 10 ...		
6 September	Louisa Johnson of Anderson – nervous	46
9 September	Benjamin Burton of Eli.	17
8 September	Thomas Lawson	4
10 September	William Hall of P. Hall, Esq.	21
	Hannah Lawson of Selby	5
21 September	James Robinson	35
3 October	Sarah Townsend Marvil wife of John P. Marvil	23
3 November	Nicey Mumford wife of John	24
7 November	Thomas Cooper (attorney)	56
	Elizabeth Palmore of W. H. Palmore	5 months
11 November	Harriett Joseph of Noah	4 weeks
5 December	Mary Truitt, Sr. – cancer	87
17 December	Elizabeth Conaway wife of Asa	40
19 December	Joseph Warrington, Sr.	65
24 or 31 December	John Martin, Sr.	54
31 December	(N) c/o Paynter Joseph	2 months
1830		
14 January	Isaiah Clifton – intem. suddenly	57
p. 11 ...		
15 January	Eliza Hill wife of John	22
17 January	Elizabeth Walls wife of Thomas – consumption	20

23 January	Solomon Dodd – intem.	40
	Elizabeth Hazzard wife of Joseph	25
	Caroline Dickerson of Peter	4
	Nancy Craig wife of David, & child (N)	28
28 January	Job Barker, Sr. – pleurisy	63
26 January	Mary Waples wife of Peter, Sr. – coleman	60
10 February	Mary Jefferson wife of William – 2 o'clock a.m.	34
13 February	John Wiltbank – major cavalry; suddenly in 7-8 hours	40
13 or 14 February	David Blocksom	63
15 February	Nancy Lingo wife of Samuel	31
21 February	Newbould Coffin	37
27 February	Joshua Burton, Jr. – chase	28
31 January or 1 February	Nathan Williams	<n/g>
25 February	Elizabeth Shirman wife of Joseph	<n/g>
9 March	Sarah Salmons wife of John & her young child (N) 2 days before	25
8 March	Patience Burton wife of Joshua	25
1 April	Nicholas Ridgely – chancellor; in 10-15 minutes	65
p. 12 ...		
5 April	Samuel Coffin	45
	John Burton of Luke	50
9 April	Thomas Burton, Sr. (collect.)	60
9 or 10 April	Johnson Riley	45

21 April	Sarah Reynold wife of Roderick	36
25-28 April	Adam Marvel, Sr.	60
29 April	Richard C. Davidson	43
5 May	Robinson Plumber – shot himself	<n/g>
10 May	Dr. Andrew C. Jackson – intem.	46
11 June	Benton Harris	64
24 June	John Wingate – drowned	45
7 July	Thomas Blizzard, Sr. – 9 o'clock p.m.	59
by 10 July	(N) Argo – drowned	<n/g>
<n/g>	a man was killed near Levin Conaway's by a horse kick	<n/g>
22 July	John Cadda – drunk	45
26 July	Isaac Morris of Jacob	25
20 July	Rev. William Hickman	67
2 August	his wife Mary	59
3 August	Josiah Cohoon – short illness	29
18 August	Thomas PettyJohn	45
7 August	Jehu Stokely	48
12 August	Mary Chase, Sr. – fever	66
11 August	Nelly Gurley	<n/g>
p. 13 ...		
12 August	Nancy Moor, Sr. – widow	66
25 August	Capt. Elisha Wharton – intem.	55
26 August	Robert Carey – hanged himself	27
11 September	Benjamin Butler	78
13 September	Nancy Wilson, Sr. widow of John	74
	Mary Rust wife of Absalom	57
	Joshua Hill of Levi	26

27 September	Mary Warrington of Joseph	38
1 October	Kendal Fowler – drowned in B. Kiln	<n/g>
	Thomas Pepper – constable	44
30 September	(N) c/o Finley Bevans	4 or 5
27 October	Anderson Johnson – billious & palsy	47
	Lucy Senscless – from sundry antil	<n/g>
30 November	Robert Torbert	35
12 December	George Pride	45
23 or 24 December	William Rhodes	35
	1831	
18 January	Louder Jones	54
22 January	Mary Coffen widow of Newbould	39
23 January	Benjamin T. Wadhams	47
30/31 January	Belinda Joseph wife of Jonathan – at midnight	69
4 February	Nathan Joseph, Sr.	73
15 January	Levin Godwin – fell from his horse (as thought) & froze to death	<n/g>
p. 14 ...		
5 February	Selby Wilson of Thomas	22
10 February	(N) c/o Elisha D. Cullen	6
	(N) c/o M. Rench, Esq.	6
16 February	Nathaniel Blizzard – 10 p.m.	37
21 February	Nathaniel Jones – drowned himself about 14 January & found in mill pond	40
24 February	(N) c/o Samuel Findal	10 weeks
25 February	David Wilson of Isaac	44
	Henry Lingo, Sr.	72

26 February	Margaret Aytes widow of William	56
	Curtis Abbott – lingering	40
7 March	Joseph Carey – midday; I. R. Hundred	68
	James Calhoon – 4 o'clock p.m.; pleurisy	35
26 March	Bersheba Burton wife of ferryman	60
	Mary Marvil – pauper	50
7 March	(N) Simpler	<n/g>
12 or 13 March	Coard Hazzard – old age	80
13 or 14 March	William Hobbs	21
	Jane Parsons of Hopkins	21
14 March	Rachel Sullivan	38
19 March	Jacob Donovan	58
31 March	Paynter Walton, Esq. – consumption	37
	John Dutten, Sr.	90
11 April	Eliza Prettyman – widow	40
p. 15 ...		
18 April	Elizabeth Goslee wife of Peter	20
17 April	Burton Johnson of Staten	24
20 May	Elizabeth Butler of Benjamin	20
22 May	Ann Kollock wife of George	38
	Paynter Waples	30
30 May	William Veazey	42
6 June	Mary Warrington wife of James – suddenly	40
11 June	Mary Wilson wife of Joshua	35
18 June	Elizabeth D. Wells wife of William H. Wells	60
21 June	Elizabeth Dagworthy Waples of W. D. W.	infant

28 June	Mary Rust wife of John	34
5 July	Hall Ennis of Samuel	25
15 July	Louiza Burton wife of Woolsey	24
22 July	Agnes Short wife of Daniel – eat huckleberries, took colic, died suddenly	40
29 July	Ebenezer Wilson – 5 o'clock p.m.	21
15 August	Robert Burton of John	21
30 August	Mary Stuart wife of John	30
2 September	John Holland of Isaac	11
	Thomas Rowland – L & R Hundred	70
	Levin Rickards	47
	James Rickards – Baltimore Hundred near Sam.	52
15 September	Mary Johnson wife of Silas	20
p. 16 ...		
12 September	Elizabeth Hudson of Wharris	24
15 September	Jeremiah Linch	35
16 evening - 17 morning September	Janille Davidson of John	16 months
23 September	Mary Bartlett wife of James	65
27 September	Katharine Jefferson wife of William	45
29 September	Rachel Morris wife of Jacob	60
3 or 4 October	Leven Lank	55
9 October	James F. Bayliss – evening	73
2 hours before 10 October	his wife Elizabeth Bayliss	74
12 October	Capt. William Harris	67
3 November	Gincey Cathell wife of Mitchell	26

4 November	Joseph Morris, Sr.	70
	Sarah Powders wife of Francis	40
13 November	John Stuart	40
5 December	Thomas Grice, Jr.	30
9 December	William Grice	22
12 December	George Robinson of Peter – by a gun	22
16 December	John Prettyman, Sr.	60
19 December	Isabella Wilson wife of Reuben	70
14 December	Susanna Lank widow of Leven	60
20 December	Albert Green	45
21 December	Roderick Reynolds – one man & family	40
22 December	Levin Dickeson	38
23 December	Sarah Dickerson wife of Edmond	60
24 December	Edmond Dickerson	65
	John Russell	40
	William Dean	45
p. 17 ...		
25 December	Samuel Carpenter	63
	Robert Waller (cryer)	55
26 December	Stephen Gerard	85
28 December	Job Goslee	60
	1832	
1 January	Jonathan Cade – drawbridge of Tudly	<n/g>
	Henrietta Meria wife of Austin – suddenly; p.m.	44
2 January	Frances Benson wife of Henry – a.m.	33
1 or 2 January	Samuel Lockwood (s. carpenter)	48
4 January	Margaret Blizzard wife of S. E.	28

6 January	Zadock Veazey, Sr. – a.m.	92
7 January	Sarah Atkins widow of Isaac – p.m.	70
9 January	Phoebe Cohoon wife of Levin & child (N)	34
	Perry Pool, Sr. – consumption; 10 p.m.	66
10 January	John McIlvaine	65
11 January	& his son (N)	<n/g>
15 January	(N) c/o Samuel B. Walls	22 hours
18 January	Katharine Burton wife of Hamilton	20
16 January	Kendal B. Atkins	39
18 or 19 January	Mary Waples widow of Robinson	49
20 January	Thomas C. Atkins – 4 o'clock p.m.	45
29 January	Dr. John Carey, Esq. – at Dover	50
1 February	Richard Palmore of William	38
2 February	Abram Wilson of Thomas	27
5 February	Joseph Dodd of John	22
8 February	John Dutten (ship carpenter) – consumption	40
p. 18 ...		
8 February	(N) Elligood wife of John	<n/g>
15 February	Sophia Burton wife of Benjamin	20
18 February	Theodore Spicer – dropsy	36
18 February	Donovan Boyar – found dead	<n/g>
24 or 25 February	Hester Mustard widow of John	58
	Deborah Marvel wife of George	24
1 March	Nancy Torbert wife of Lawrence	24
4 March	Richard Bloxum s/o Richard	20
2 March	Mary Ingraim wife of John	30

9 or 10 March	Elizabeth Ann Holland wife of Elisha	23
10 March	Lenna Beauchamp wife of William	30
16 March	Dr. Joseph Marsh	60
17 March	(N) Hall wife of Purnall (wheelwright, Milford)	40
23 March	Mary Simpler wife of Thomas	5 [sic]
20 March	Francis Powders	52
	& wife (N) – sometime before, say 5 months	<n/g>
29 March	Benjamin Francklin	50
20 April	Purnal Tindal (sheriff)	70
20 April	John Massey	42
18 April	& his wife (N)	43
p. 19 ...		
1 May	Nancy Goslee widow of Job	56
18 or 19 April	Sarah Dutten widow of Thomas	60
25 or 26 April	Sarah Dutten widow of John	70
2 or 3 May	Unice Dutton widow of Nol. (?)	70
17 May	Milloway Write – at Creek; sudden	60
29 May	Kendal S. Coffin	22
5 June	Nancy Lingo wife of Henry	45
7 June	Isaac Messick – old age	70
28 June	Hezekiah Joseph, Sr.	70
5 July	William Parsons	50
22 July	Thomas Reynolds	56
5 September	Rhoda Spicer widow of Curtis	52
4 or 5 September	William Burton (ferryman)	8 [sic]
29 October	Henry P. Fisher	45

27 October	Sally Palmore wife of Jonathan	25
4 November	Sarah Walls wife of Eli	26
5 November	Joseph Godwin	60
28 November	Dr. Robert Burton	41
7 December	Mary Walker wife of James	28
10 or 11 December	(N) wife of Edward Richards	25
12 December	Derick Bernard, Esq.	40
15 December	Sarah Hill wife of Levi	62
23 December	Robert Morris of Zipporah	2
27 December	Mary Johnson wife of Richard	63
1833		
1 January	John Spicer, Esq.	63
27 January	Nancy Wine wife of William	30
28 or 29 January	Samuel Warrington	42
p. 20 ...		
22 January	Samuel Johnson (clerk)	24
13 February	Jehu Lawson	39
14 February	Elisha Holstein	50
	Howard, Mary, & Sally Holstein – within about 2 months past; same family	<n/g>
28 February	Asa Conaway	40
10 March	Wrixham Lewis	42
21 June	Elizabeth (N) c/o Richard	8 months
12 June	George Roach	25
June or July	Ruth wife of Isaac Waples	<n/g>
19 June	(N) Prettyman wife of Warren	40

15 July	(N) c/o David Steward	3
	Peter Hopkins	2
11 or 20 July	Polly Warrington (butcher's widow)	65
21 July	Elizabeth wife of James Anderson	37
5 August	Robert Evans	53
24 or 25 August	Richard Simpler	40
7 September	John Way, Esq.	60
9 September	Elizabeth Wright (widow)	60
20 September	Mary (late Joseph) wife of Isaac Hall	22
5 October	John Rowland of Paynter	50
8 October	John Robinson Lingo – drowned	33
9 October	Sarah Stokely of Jehu	23
24 or 25 October	3 people killed at once – near Garrettson McCabe, his sons, one negro	18
		21
		<n/g>
3 November	Hezekiah Lacey	68 or 73
p. 21 ...		
5 November	Rhoda widow of Robert Lacey	69
	George Truitt, Esq. – Baltimore	<n/g>
7 December	Nancy d/o Burton Walls	4
	Benjamin Pool – Warwick, drowned	30
8 December	William Goslee, Sr.	53
15 December	Capt. Thomas Scott – fall from a horse	38
	1834	
9 or 10 January	Eliza Ann Burton of Coroll	21
12 January	Joseph Draper (s. carpenter)	2 [sic]
3 March	Mary Toomy (widow)	68

4 March	Susan Carey wife of Thomas	30
	Lany Prettyman of Emory	15
5 March	Rev. John Mitchelmore	46
	John Middleton (Negro)	<n/g>
8 March	Eve Chase wife of William	40
18 March	Nancy Lawles wife of Stephen – consumption	38
15 March	John Collins (late sheriff)	47
6 or 7 May	Gilbert Pool	39
10 May	David Craig	30
12 May	Zechariah Reynolds	72
20 May	William Lank of William	18
23 May	Robert Hanson s/o Minah – fell in a hole clamming & drowned	16
	4 or 5 Blacks drowned off against Lewiston – Richard Wesley in taking them in as runaways	<n/g>
13 June	Lettce Walls wife of Purnal	21
14 June	Perry s/o William Pool	7 months
20 June	Edward Harmon	75
16 or 20 June	(N) c/o John Lingo	2 weeks
26 or 27 June	(N) wife of E. L. Wills	24
24 or 25 June	Joseph Carey (Milton)	57
p. 22 ...		
2 July	George Robinson, Sr.	69
3 July	Nancy Walker wife of Thomas	55
8 or 9 July	Thomas Shirman, Sr.	68
10 July	James Holland – by thunder	12
28 July	Ruth Coalter	60

22 July	James C. Johnson of Perry	17 months
18 July	Mary Baily widow of Aaron	55
25 July	Samuel Lingo – 8 o'clock a.m.; consumption	39
5 August	Thomas Joseph s/o Hezekiah – 9 days sick	25
1 August	Alice Paynter (widow)	42
9 August	William Argus (blacksmith)	25
10 August	Anna Hall widow of Edward	63
29 September	Nutter Lofland	45
4 October	Isaac Jester s/o Daniel	3
19 or 20 October	Priscilla Warren	12
25 October	Horatio Collins	69
27 October	Josiah Hopkins	65
10 November	Samuel Evans – brother of Nancy	30
14 November	Elizabeth Johnson – 3 o'clock a.m.	61
16 November	Mary Hamilton wife of Purnal	25
4 December	Samuel Johnson, Sr. – 1 o'clock p.m.	60
6 December	Theodore W. Joseph – 9 o'clock a.m.	18 months
	Young Walls of David of N.	20 days
8 December	John Williams (Millsboro)	56
10 December	& wife	50
15 December	Abram Reynolds	39
28 December	George Polk	50
22 December	Nancy Harper (widow)	<n/g>
26 December	John Harper	30

p. 23 ...		
28 December	William Pool	30
	1835	
8 January	Elizabeth Kollock widow of Philip	65
16 January	Cornelia Dodd wife of Asahel	25
16 to 20 January	Isabella Butcher wife of Derick	60
	Leuranah Simpson wife of Purnal	70
	Susanna Houston wife of Shepherd	25
27 or 28 January	Peter Hall, Esq.	60
28 January	William J. Coffin	45
2 February	Hester wife of James Bartlett	25
3 February	William Polite	50
9 February	Purnal Walls	30
10 February	J. Backer Handy (Negro)	47
20 February	Dixon Harris	65
1 March	William Wardle	40
28 February	Samuel Walls – 10 p.m.	64
8 March	(N) Mcally wife of (N) Mcally, Esq.	<n/g>
6 March	Luke Lamb	50
13 March	(N) Rust c/o Thomas – scalded	5
27 March	William M. Connelly of Jane	25
31 March	William Lank	<n/g>
1 April	Mary wife of John Salmons	30
7 April	Asa Warren	40
	Sally wife of Woolsey Hall	<n/g>
5 April	Jonathan Joseph, Sr. – ¼ before 2 p.m.	73
	Edy widow of Jos. Morris	72

9 April	Mary wife of George Marvel	22
	~~William Palmore~~	
17 April	Woolsey Pride	49
22 April	Mary wife of William Benson	25
p. 24 ...		
19 May	Elisha Pennywell	40
11 June	Lettee Hurdle – 4 o'clock a.m.	17
7 March	Tamar Dukes (widow)	<n/g>
	Purnall Short, Jr.	27
14 July	Thomas Hobbs – hanged himself	60
17 August	William Jefferson of Warren	60
1 September	Burton Morris of Thomas	31
31 August	John Short brother of Philip	50
9 or 10 September	Isaac Lofland	54
15 September	Adaline wife of Benjamin Burton, Esq.	<n/g>
15-18 September	Sarah A. wife of J. H. Harris	<n/g>
27 or 28 September	Joseph Reed (Milton)	46
12 October	Kezia wife of Stephen Blizzard – 5 a.m.	68
8 or 9 October	Purnal Simpson	66
16 October	Sally wife of William Parsons	53
24 October	Hester wife of William B. Blizzard	37
1 November	Letty widow of Theodore Spicer	40
17 November	(N) wife of Coventon Messick	70
18 November	John Smith nephew of David – suddenly	19
26 November	Sarah wife of John P. Palmore	43
3 December	Rebecca wife of Peter Parker	55

5 December	Nancy c/o John Finall of Purnall – burnt	2
27 December	Aora Dodd	69
31 December	Jehu Warrington	50
25 December	(N) Adams – shot in Dover	<n/g>
	Lydia Davis of Samuel	8
	1836	
10 January	Nancy widow of Asa Warren	24
8 January	Sarah Ann Davis of Samuel	1
11 January	Mary wife of James Bailey	41
11 February	John Pool of Perry – pleurisy	23
	John H. Blizzard of Levin	16 months
p. 25 ...		
26 February	Joseph H. Warrington – 11 o'clock a.m.	13
29 February	Robert Hunter – 5 o'clock p.m.	6
26 February	William Gray – froze	<n/g>
4 March	William King	23
	& his sister	<n/g>
9 March	Isaac Dennis	40
	Charles King	52
12 March	William J. Harris	38
30 March	Elzey Palmore, Sr.	44
31 March	Martha Justus – not dead	40
	~~& children~~	<n/g>
	Abel PettyJohn	<n/g>
2 April	Burton Donovan	30
7 April	Abel PettyJohn	25
8 April	William Jacobs	<n/g>

13 April	Thomas Wingate	56
	Anna Warrington	5
15 or 16 April	Lettee wife of John Conner	<n/g>
	Aaron Marvel, Sr.	66
	(N) Burton wife of Isaiah	60
28 April	John Parker, Sr.	67
1 May	Jesse Passwaters	56
3 May	May wife of Joseph Males	25
9 May	Caleb P. Bennett (governor)	70
11 May	(N) wife of Richard Waller – childbed	<n/g>
20 May	Penelope wife of Josiah Dutton	44
26 May	Peter Robinson (judge)	6 [sic]
7 August	Heensy Hopkins	25
p. 26 ...		
7 August	Margaret c/o William J. Harris	<n/g>
15 August	Thomas Rust, Sr.	62
22 August	Henrietta Jane c/o Brinkly Johnson	10
	Caleb Johnson c/o Nelson Johnson	2
4 September	Thomas Marvel, Sr.	76
August	John Blizzard	30
6 or 7 October	Selby Lawson, Sr. – midnight	50
6 October	Mary wife of William Mgee	33
10 October	John West, Sr.	96 years 9 months
15 October	Rachel wife of Abram Wilson – a.m.	60
10 October	Gideon s/o William Joseph, Jr.	7
	Lemuel Walls – 5 o'clock a.m.; sick 6 weeks	26

7 November	Nancy widow of William Harris, Sr.	66
12 November	Tabitha wife of Benjamin McIlvaine	23
7 November	(N) child burnt to death at home of William Spicer – clothes caught fire	7
4 November	James [sic] wife of John Burton (carriagemaker)	41
16 November	(N) c/o S. R. Wilson	1
22 – 26 November	James Starr	43
near 1st December	Scofield Rodney	60
18 or 19 December	(N) Duskey or Drisco (shoemaker, Georgetown)	<n/g>
21 December	Thomas Heath	60
22 December	Henry Sharp	38
23 or 24 December	Gideon Walls of James	19
29 December	Sarah wife of Noah Joseph – suddenly	33
19 December	William Futcher (Rehoboth)	70
1837		
12 or 15 January	3 people (N) at Milsboro	<n/g>
p. 27 ...		
13 February	John Buckle of Joseph	16
19 February	Alfred R. Spicer of Sarah	6
	John Linch	25
1 March	(N) wife of Richard Dutten	27
	Mary Davis d/o Nelea	18

7 March	(N) Gordy mother of Aaron	<n/g>
	Thomas G. West – 12 to 1 o'clock; at Milton, measles	38
13 March	Aaron Gordy – 2 o'clock a.m.	3
28 March	Mary wife of Zechariah Joseph	70
23 March	(N) c/o Levin Blizzard	4 months
19 March	Woolsey H. Palmore, Jr. of William	19
1 April	William c/o William Palmore	1
3 April	John Mumford	33
	George Prettyman of Stephen	19
9 April	Samuel Walls of Samuel – 6 a.m.	2
15 April	(N) wife of Dr. S. K. Wilson	38
last of April	Stephen Hill, Esq.	50
13 May	Martha Ann Jefferson – measles; 20 minutes after 11 o'clock p.m.	18
10 May	(N) c/o Isaac Bartlett	5
14 May	& wife Sarah	30
	John Holland (carpenter)	30
1 June	(N) widow of James Stan	26
9 June	Martha Wilson of Richard – measles	32
10 July	(N) wife of E. D. Wells, Esq.	22
11 July	Abel Thomas – Baltimore	62
p. 28 ...		
25 July	George F. Simple of P.	5
7 or 8 August	Robert c/o Azel Johnson	4
8 or 9 August	(N) c/o Nelson Johnson	1
8 September	Maria wife of William B. Morris	40
	William Coffin of Jordan	17

19 October	John Davidson – suddenly; sick not 1 day	43
11 October	Levi Hopkins – hanged	40
8 November	Peter Goslee of William	30
11 November	(N) c/o Jonathan J. Wilson	10 hours
20 November	Eleanor Palmore, Sr.	60
29 November	Lettee widow of William Veasey	48
	Prudence wife of John Palmore	45
1838		
7 February	Capt. John Craig (Milton)	<n/g>
8 February	Patience Stokely – old age	76
7 February	Thomas Lank	65
9 February	Patience wife of Samuel Joseph of J.	43
12 or 13 March	Mitchel Virden	72
13 March	Nancy wife of William Simple	25
1 March	Henry Lingo of Henry	53
19 March	Wallace Waples	68
	Joshua Wilson	50
5 April	Joseph Prettyman	50
11 April	Derickson Butcher	60
12 April	Hester wife of Thomas D. Shirman	40
14 or 15 April	Abram Read	65
about 25 April	John Hood	60
30 April or 1 May	David Mustard (musician)	65
8 or 10 May	William Mcgee	50
15 or 20 May	Kendal Batson	65
April or May	William Freeman – suddenly	<n/g>
p. 29 ...		

5 June	Comfort widow of Derickson Butcher	40
11 June	William Jefferson of Job	55
15 June	Miss (N) Maull at Lewes	<n/g>
July	Levi Cannon (lawyer)	66
9 August	George Bennum, Sr. – drowned	51
1 or 2 August	Nancy wife of Gilley Short	50
11 or 12 August	Samuel Watson (Milton) – by cart wheel	5
25 August	Mary Simpler (Sharp)	49
24 August	William Benson – deep cold	35
27 August	William B. Spicer, Sr.	65
	(N) d/o William Vent	17
28 August	(N) of John Palmore	<n/g>
5 September	Rev. John Conwell	62
	Isaac F. Griffith – consumption	26
17 September	Levi Hill – lingering	75
19 September	Elizabeth c/o C. G. Rigely, Esq. – by a fall	19 months
10 September	Stephen s/o Jacob Wilson – bite or sting	12
16 September	Theodore Hudson – by fall from horse	27
21 or 22 October	William S. Hazzard	38
30 or 31 October	Peter Waples	71
12 November	Myers Brerton – evening	60
	Thomas Foster	<n/g>
22 November	Margaret Warrington	59
24 or 25 December	George Hobbs	30

26 December	Lovey Johnson	50
p. 30	**1839**	
27 January	Mary Fleetwood	50
26 January	Hannah W. d/o S. W. Johnson	3 months
12 January	Mary widow of Philip W. Meriner – not dead	60
6 February	Sarah Ann wife of William S. Joseph	21
25 February	Zadock Hartt	35
22 February	Dr. Wilbur Fisk	<n/g>
about 1 March	Sophia Tull	48
2 March	(N) c/o Dr. G. W. Maull	<n/g>
4 March	Mark Davis (Prime Hook)	65
22 March	(N) c/o John Medley Wolf – drowned	2
4 May	Samuel B. Walls	31 years 6 days
	John Rust	38
6 May	Elizabeth wife of Richard Johnson	51
8 May	(N) black child of George Frame	<n/g>
1 June	(N) s/o Forctwell Wright	24
5 June	(N) wife of Mitchell Lank	<n/g>
9 June	Jane wife of Thomas Grice	70
20 August	(N) c/o Nelson Johnson	<n/g>
26 August	(N) c/o N. D. Welsh	1
25 August	Ann wife of James A. Harris	37
	(N) widow of Peter Robinson (judge)	60
	Purnal Short, Sr.	65
1 September	Samuel Parker (Georgetown)	32
5 September	Abraham Nelson	63

21 October	James Johnson – 2 o'clock a.m.; consumption	54
3 October	(N) wife of James Steel	30
	James R. Black (judge)	50
November	Joseph Willson	25
9 November	George W. Atkins of William	13
p. 31 ...		
	Chloe Philips sister of Benjamin Cannon	<n/g>
15 December	Joshua Ingram – suddenly	32
	Mary Conaway (widow)	42
24 December	Dr. S. R. Wilson – consumption	45
28 December	Eleanor Marvel – sick long	70
	1840	
5 or 6 January	Rev. Daniel Jester	83
31 January	Saby widow of Woolsey Burton	50
5 February	George Rogers	66
7 February	Eliza wife of Elisha Lingo	42
10 February	David C. Walls – long illness	30
14 February	Levin Conaway – old age	98
15 February	John C. Burton – consumption	28
21 February	John Hopkins	55
23 February	John Conwell	74
24 February	Elizabeth wife of John Palmore – sick 9 years	73
18 February	Mary d/o John Thorogood	30
	Mary d/o Ed. Vickars	<n/g>
23 February	Nancy d/o James Cohoon	13
1 March	Mary Anne Maclin d/o Peter Cohoon	11

22 March	Elizabeth widow of Thomas G. West	40
	Charles Henry c/o N. W. Walls	3
27 February	(N) c/o William D. Waples, Jr.	2 weeks
20 February	John Burbbayge	70
p. 32 ...		
28 March	Jane wife of William D. Waples	20
8 April	Ellis Wright (Fretwell)	2
1 April	news of death of Eli Carey in West	<n/g>
	Ashbel Strong (Lewistown)	<n/g>
27 April	(N) c/o Noah Joseph	7 days
10 May	William D. Cannon – suddenly	28
10 to 15 May	(N) Shockley – from cold fishing	<n/g>
12 to 18 July	John Lingo of Jesse	26
19 September	Asbury c/o James B. Joseph	1 or 2
19 October	Joshua Johnson	40
23 October	Peter s/o Eber Torbert	15
	John Dorman	52
13 October	Mariah wife of John Prettyman	25
3 November	George Pepper	28
~~4 November~~	~~Eliza wife of J. R. Barker~~	~~42~~
5 November	Asa Johnson – 6 o'clock a.m.; leader for 37 years	61
2 November	Patience wife of Gideon Walls	30
21 November	Lydia widow of Jehu Warrington	54
30 November	Sarah wife of Peter Walls	60
28 December	Burton Joseph – suddenly; consumption	28
30 December	John R. Evans	33
1841		

2 January	William Conwell	70
31 December	(N) wife of John Conwell	70
10 January	Hannah wife of Joseph Oliver (Georgetown)	<n/g>
p. 33 ...		
22 January	(N) c/o Joseph Marvel	1
8 February	(N) c/o George W. Joseph	4 days
6 February	Elijah Hudson (C. Creek Hundred)	60
10 February	James Wilson (BeeThe)	28
13 February	Elizabeth widow of Myers Biston	50
14 February	Edmund Dean	<n/g>
11 March	Elizabeth Hazzard widow of Alias Hazzard	50
24 March	Lydia d/o Henry Lingo	<n/g>
4 April	Gen. W. H. Harrison (president) – half past 12 a.m. Sunday	68 & 2 months
9 April	Zachariah PettyJohn – inebriate	40
	Gideon Hunter – drowned in Broad Kiln Creek about 2 a.m.	23
1 April	Mr. (N) Dewasle (Milford) – drink	<n/g>
9 or 10 April	Elihu Thorogood	60
4 April	Sarah wife of James Simpler – 1 o'clock a.m.; sick 5 weeks	53
16 April	Eliza d/o Davis Walls	5
26 April	Ann wife of John Prettyman	26
	(N) c/o Robert L. Johnson	1 day
27 April	(N) c/o Nath. M. Johnson	7 days
5 June	Eliza wife of James Tindal	<n/g>
	Nancy wife of Robert Johnson	28

about 27 May	Gabriel Riley – suicide	65
9 June	Sophia Ann Connelly d/o James & Ann M. Walls – ½ past 4 o'clock p.m.; 4 hours illness	19
16 June	Leah wife of James Rust	25
4 July	Nancy wife of Brinkley Johnson – 9 o'clock afternoon & 20 minutes	50
18 July	Elizabeth wife of Thomas Joseph of Samuel	24
25 July	Henry O. Bannum (Paisy)	75½
9 August	Nehemiah Lofland	60
27 August	Elizabeth wife of William Palmore – lingering	70
p. 34 ...		
last of August	Eliza Ann d/o James Tindal	3 months
about 1 September	George Bell (Lewes & Rehoboth)	28
27 September	John Fausky – suddenly	<n/g>
9 October	Adaline Ennis of Purnal	21
11 October	William s/o David Moore	3
19 October	Col. William D. Waples	65
20 October	Elizabeth wife of Nehemiah Walls	57
31 October	John Burrows (Milton) – some deaf	50
15 November	Isaac Jones brother to William	<n/g>
13 or 14 November	Lewicy d/o William Wilson	4
20 November	Joseph Evans (Milton)	32
29 November	Kendal Marvel – 3 o'clock a.m.	39 or 40
	Joseph Mails (mason) – intemperatence	36

4 December	Ann wife of John West – D. L. Walls	24
16 December	Elizabeth Waller sister of Robert (dec'd)	60
19 December	(N) c/o James Walls of Thomas	4 days
22 December	George H. Atkins	56 years 1 month
	James Ward (C. Creek)	<n/g>
	William Ward – left family, widow (N) & son (N)	30 odd
	Jacob Mase	35
1842		
3 January	Nancy widow of Burton Joseph	55
6 January	Edward P. Walton (Georgetown)	11
30 January	Burton Lingo – suddenly; by horse	26
12 February	Mariam Dodd	60
	Sally Christopher (widow)	55
13 February	Jane Benky (McIlvaine) – by fire	60
p. 35 ...		
18 February	Lydia wife of John Marvel	30
20 February	Comfort widow of William Clark	7 [sic]
25 February	William Peckerton	45
about 20 March	James Short – staff of timber cast	<n/g>
25 March	Eustic James Spicer	6
27 March	Joshua Morris	57
1 May	Rachel Burbbayge	20
6 June	Robert McFerrin Johnson	9 months
13 June	(N) c/o L. L. Lyons	1
14 June	(N) c/o James PettyJohn	<n/g>
3 July	(N) c/o Robert Warrington	<n/g>

11 July	(N) c/o William Wilson of E.	<n/g>
16 July	& 3 or 4 more was dead in Georgetown & more dying as believed & several more in Milton	<n/g>
17 July	John West (Milsboro) – an old woman [sic] – suddenly	<n/g>
22 July	David Hazzard (Angola)	70
27 July	Belinda wife of Jacob Hurdle	52
27 or 28 July	Sarah d/o John Davidson	17
29 or 30 July	(N) c/o Nelson Johnson	13 months
9 August	Sarah wife of George Prettyman	20
7 August	Peter Spicer	38
1 September	Eli Walls, Sr.	67
9 September	Sarah wife of John Salmon	30
	Sarah wife of Edward Burton	20
	Mary wife of James Bartlett	27
7 or 8 September	Jane Valentine	<n/g>
p. 36 ...		
	2 children (N) of Silas Smith	<n/g>
18 September	Coard Burton	5
about 22 September	David Marvel	<n/g>
28 September	Nancy d/o Zachariah Bunnum	6
7 October	Margaret wife of Cornelius Mustard	<n/g>
3 November	Zechariah Joseph	76
15 November	Jane wife of Stephen Morris	75

10 or 15 November	Josiah Martin	70
5 December	Hannah Dodd (Sand Hills) – 6 o'clock a.m.	53
	Elizabeth wife of Robert Warren – 6 o'clock a.m.	49
8 December	John Wilson s/o Elzey	16
18 December	George P. Anderson	24
16 December	David Baily – small pox	22
1843		
4 January	Hold Wilson widow of Thomas	60
	William Kendrick & wife (N)	<n/g>
26 December	James Bailey – small pox	56
9 January	Nancy wife of James Roach	30
	Mary Hudson – at B. McIlvaine	30
11 January	John Brinkloe (lawyer)	35
3 February	Mary wife of Robert Waples	50
11 February	Thomas Grice, Sr.	80
6 March	John C. Davis (L court)	35
21 March	Parker Robinson	68
2 March	Daniel Burton of Daniel	24
15 March	William C. c/o Coard Warrington	4
3 April	Mary wife of Peter Walls – 9 o'clock a.m.	49
8 April	Jacob Cannon – murder; 1 day ill	68
5 May	Isaac Cannon	70 odd
10 May	(N) wife of (N) West & her daughter (N)	<n/g>
p. 37 ...		

<no date>	(N) c/o William Jefferson of William	<n/g>
	(N) c/o Robert Jefferson, Jr.	<n/g>
19 May	(N) Way wife of E. J. Way (preacher)	2 [sic]
27 May	Joseph Wilson, Sr. – ill but 2 hours	72
21 May	Sophia Ann d/o Brinkley L. Walls – ill 6 or 7 weeks, oft very bad	2 months 1 day
8 May	Noah Webster, Esq. – of spelling book	60
30 June	John Prettyman of Ann	36
4 July	Louder Layton, Jr.	24
22 July	Richard West	50
	Mark Davis	<n/g>
	John W. Dean	<n/g>
23 July	(N) wife of Daniel Burton of D.	20
	a black boy (N)	13
30 July	(N) wife of Capt. John Waples	23
6 or 7 August	Charles Fisher	3
26 August	Molton Rickards – 10 o'clock p.m.	60 odd
8 September	Thomas D. Shirman	36
5 September	Alexander Warrington s/o Alexander	8
10 September	Robert Warrington his brother	17
10 or 11 September	Robert McFerran	50
15 September	Robert Henry s/o Elzey Palmore	2 years 3 months
16 September	Sarah wife of Jonathan Messeck	62
12 September	Josiah Cannon	50
13 September	Capt. Isaac Bradley – against break water; vessel raised & the body of Bradley 14 days after in the cabin	<n/g>

25 September	Louiza d/o Dag Derrickson	18
p. 38 ...		
23 September	Patience wife of Samuel Brereton	60
	Ann wife of John Steet	35
	Sarah wife of Robert Warrington	28
24 September	(N) c/o William Rickards	<n/g>
30 September	(N) c/o William Rickards	<n/g>
28 September	Chloe wife of Eli Pepper	50
29 September	Thomas Robinson, Esq. – justice of high law court	62
4 October	2 children (N) of William Goslee of Lettee	<n/g>
3 or 4 October	William West	25
3 October	(N) c/o Richard Bloxom	10
4 October	(N) c/o Richard Bloxom	7
	Mary Ellen d/o R. Warrington	1
	2 children (N) of Amos Simpler – in 2 weeks	<n/g>
7 October	Elihu Joseph, Sr.	65
2 October	Joseph Linch	45
4 or 5 October	Benjamin West	30
9 October	Robert L. Harris – 7 o'clock p.m.	55
13 October	Arcada wife of Eli Walls of Eli	26
	(N) s/o Bowen Harman	<n/g>
27 October	Rachel c/o H. O. Bennum	1
28 October	Thomas Robinson (lawyer) – long illness	44
6 November	William Perry of James	40
	(N) wife of David Richards	<n/g>
25 November	John Cade – fell dead; ebriety	38

1 December	Mary wife of Zadoc Milby	40
5 December	James Hudson	26
11 December	Kittury Jefferson	<n/g>
5 December	(N) wife of Jessee Walls	30
25 November	Mary wife of George Bennett	24
30 November	John s/o Poel Ennis	21
14 December	Joshua Barton, Esq.	79
p. 39 ...		
15 December	Ann wife of John West (merchant)	30
	Sarah widow of Mitchell Scott (Georgetown)	80
~~16 December~~	~~Ann widow of George Bell~~	~~35~~
29 December	Elizabeth widow of Minos Wilson	48
	(N) wife of Philip Short (farmer, Dagsboro)	<n/g>
	1844	
5 to 10 January	4 colored people died, viz: Ishmael, wife (N) of Mitchell Rigware, 1 at Milton, & 1 perhaps at Milsborough	<n/g>
12 January	Henry Lingo (blacksmith)	50
1 February	John Thoroughgood	52
	John Thorogood of William	34
4 January	Samuel Walls of Thomas – 9 o'clock a.m.	50
6 January	Lydia Hester d/o Wallace	4
7 January	Spencer Phillips	35
	John C. David (Cedar Creek)	<n/g>
	Tabitha wife of Kendal Donovan	39

5 February	William Henry s/o Samuel Wallis of Burton	4
12 February	Joseph Brown s/o Elizabeth & John	<n/g>
	(N) Collins (widow), stepmother of D. Hazzard	70
	George Messeck (miller)	20
15 February	Woolsey Burton	40
16 February	William Howell (apprentice, Millsboro)	19
4 March	John Lawles, Sr. – near Ed. Marvel	60
	(N) c/o Thomas B. Sipple	1
9 March	Riley s/o Jacob Wilson – scalded	3
15 March	William Coffen – Slaughter Neck; January class leader	55
8 March	George Parker, Jr.	55
17 March	Gardiner W. Warrington	34
p. 40 ...		
19 March	Ann J. wife of Jacob Fossett	40
20 or 21 March	Sarah Ann Warrington – about midnight	16
January	Benjamin Burton (Torbert)	37
	John s/o Levi Short	12
13 April	Eliza widow of John Cade	36
18 April	Leurana wife of William Reynolds	28
25 April	Sarah Ann wife of J. S. Layton	35
26 April	George Paynter (Negro)	<n/g>
1 May	Rev. Joseph Lybrand	51
22 May	Mary widow of James Lawson	71
	a man (N) killed near Laurel by the wind breaking off the top of chimney which fell on him.	<n/g>

26 May	Robert William Prettyman	55
27 May	Emiretta wife of Samuel Barber	20
30 May	Nancy wife of Rhodes Wilson	22
2 June	Ebenezer PettyJohn, Jr.	40
2 July	Nancy Emily Sandsburg d/o B. L. Mace	2 months
	(N) c/o Jacob Kimmey	3 weeks
5 July	Adaline d/o John Kollock	15
Spring	Somerset Dickerson	50
11 July	Eliza wife of Leonard Short (Dutton)	40
15 July	Charles G. Ridgely, Esq.	38
21 July	Adam Burton	40
25 July	Rev. William Bag. Burton	62
9 August	Rev. William Connelly	40
p. 41 ...		
16 August	Leonard Short (Dutten)	48
18 August	Purnal Johnson	50
	Leuranah Bowlin (Cannon) – Rehob.	60
19 August	John Lawlis – sudden	35
11 to 17 August	reports say 10 persons died last week in Bridgeville	<n/g>
1 September	John Wilson of Josh.	47
4 September	Thomas Burbbayge	33
7 September	Sophia wife of David Hopkins	36
11 September	Elizabeth widow of James Johnson – ½ past 8 a.m.	<n/g>
12 September	Elizabeth d/o Nelson L. Johnson	5
17 September	William Johnson, Sr. – 10 o'clock	78 wanting 30 hours

14 September	Joseph Neal of John (hog)	17
15 September	Joseph Alford s/o Alexander Warring – 1 o'clock a.m.	7
16 September	Robert S. Bennum – 1 o'clock a.m.	27
10 September	George Abbott	<n/g>
8 September	Dagworthy s/o Dag Derickson	<n/g>
3 or 6 October	John Hays (Prime Hook)	60
21 September	Ann C. wife of Robert Marine	44
4 (evening) or 5 (morning) October	her child (N)	3 weeks
13 October	twin children (N) of John W. Shockley	4
12 October	Catharine d/o Wools H. Palmore	24
21 October	Beniah Watson, Esq.	55
10 October	Mary wife of Simon Spearman (auditor)	<n/g>
24 October	Parker Morris – by a fall	5
	Jane Cord (Dagsboro) – hanged herself	30
p. 42 ...		
24 October	Hester c/o Zach Bennum	4
1 November	Leven Vaughan (levy court)	48
	Nathan Harmon – colored man	<n/g>
4 November	Mary wife of Thomas Draper, Sr. – 1 & 2 o'clock a.m.	78
	(N) wife of Thomas Draper, Jr.	<n/g>
	Mary widow of John Hays	<n/g>
28 November	Lydia Ann wife of William Shockley	16
8 November	Capt. Joshua Bennet	44
10 December	Diademia wife of Samuel Flowers	40
	Sarah Jane wife of Isaac Wilson (Reed)	18

12 or 13 December	Samuel Flowers	48
13 December	Zipporah wife of Thomas A. Jones	40
23 December	(N) widow of Philip Jones	<n/g>
29 December	James Morris of Step.	49
24 December	John Parker of P. P. (Milton)	22
22 December	James P. Lofland – const.	45
31 December	Josiah H. Smith (Rich)	50
1845		
10 January	George Short – murdered	<n/g>
12 January	John Palmore, Sr.	79
25 January	Lewis Spicer	60
30 January	Sarah A. wife of Theodore Marvel	22
	(N) s/o Meshach Elliot	13
	Sarah widow of Phil. Donavan	20
1 February	Sarah wife of Nehemiah Dorman	35
4 February	Elizabeth wife of Gideon Wall	27
p. 43 ...		
5 February	(N) wife of Philip Short	30
25 January	Elizabeth wife of Robert Williams	<n/g>
6 February	George Benson	35
5 February	James PettyJohn of E.	51
31 January	Caleb Cirwithen	52
1 February	Hannah Wright	35
2 February	Eliza d/o Bevan Cellonis	30
11 February	Hester widow of Nehemiah Bennett	87
21 February	Elizabeth Brittenham	5
	James S. Dutten	48

23 February	(N) wife of Wingate Donavan	24
	~~James Parker~~	~~5~~
9 March	Isaac Meloney	52
28 February	James s/o Henry Sharp	19
2 March	Edward Vickars	50
5 March	Mary Walls d/o Thomas	50
	Ann widow of Woolsey Waples	60
1 March	Mary widow of David Truit	70
8 March	Mary widow of William Pierce	50
15 March	Joseph Houston (Georgetown)	65
27 or 28 March	John M. West, Esq. (Lewes)	6 [sic]
1 April	Mary wife of Thomas Wilson (Pool)	48
23 April	Lydia wife of James Prettyman (carp)	56
27 April	Hester wife of Peter Simpler	19
	Purnal Johnson (Annanias) – lightning lodged tree	23
26 April	(N) Carlisle (St. Johnstown)	13
p. 44 ...		
19 May	Albert Holland – drowned	28
26 May	Mary Maranda c/o Renatus T. Walls	3 months
27 May	(N) s/o John Prettyman	2 months
	& (N) c/o Wallace Veasey	<n/g>
28 May	Mary Ann of Noah Joseph	7 months
25 May	(N) c/o Nathaniel Burton	<n/g>
1 May	Hester wife of John Bennett (Leader)	54
30 May	Hester wife of Elisha Carey	30
8 June	2 children (N) of Benjamin McIlvaine	<n/g>
16 June	Arthur Milby	64

17 June	(N) c/o Bayard Joseph	<n/g>
8 June	Gen. Andrew Jackson – 6 o'clock p.m.	79
18 June	Rachel wife of Leven Calhoon	40
9 August	John P. Paynter of Samuel	34
25 August	John W. Palmore – sick 6 months	47
	Penelope Prettyman	60
5 September	Hetty widow of R. S. Bennum	24
4 September	Anna wife of William Reese	70
13 September	George Frame – 4 o'clock a.m.	49
	Peter Harris – insane	56
20 September	Simon K. Wilson	19
21 September	Margaret wife of Samuel P. Wilson	19
20 September	(N) d/o William Rider (ross)	girl
27 September	William Palmore	89
6 October	Samuel Paynter	79
p. 45 ...		
16 October	Woolsey Hall – suddenly	55
24 October	Mary Ann d/o Robert Warren	17
25 October	Margaret Parker d/o George – consumption	15
	William Abdill	30
31 October	Nancy widow of Burton Morris – lingering	78
23 November	William Beachamp	54
24 November	Warren Prettyman (Georgetown)	70
26 November	Elizabeth wife of Josiah Ben	24
27 November	George Robinson (Baltimore)	<n/g>
23 November	Elizabeth widow of Thomas Riley (Slaughter Neck)	60

9 December	Elizabeth widow of John Burbbayge – after long illness	56
	~~Benjamin Dorey~~	~~35~~
20 December	George Messick	40
21 December	Ebenezer Joseph	60
22 December	Gust. A. Ewing, Esq. (Slore)	55
	Capt. Paul Waples	70
26 December	Rachel widow of Thomas Blizzard	73
28 December	Capt. Salathiel Baker	40
29 December	Amy wife of William C. Joseph	29
	Adam Burton	40
24 December	(N) c/o Peter Dodd	4 days
26 December	George Hearn	55
	1846	
8 January	Benjamin McIlvaine of Jane	36
8 December	Sarah wife of Mitchell Scott	40
12 January	Benjamin Johnson	80
14 January	Daniel Brereton, Esq.	50
p. 46 ...		
18 January	Heavilow Morris	40
5 January	William Goslee of William	35
	Mary widow of James Rickards	<n/g>
4 January	Maria Catharine d/o George Hall (Milton)	16
	Mary widow of Charles Fisher	<n/g>
16 February	Robert of John Spicer	<n/g>
	(N) apprentice of John Marvel	16

24 February	Jacob Sharp, Sr.	70
	Maria widow of William Stephenson	49
	Sarah widow of William Polite	55
2 March	Thomas Stockton (governor)	67
	Myra Kollock	<n/g>
6 or 7 March	Richard Salmons – 3 a.m.	35
10 March	Charles Wyatt (constable)	30
22 March	James Warrington – 2 o'clock Sunday morning	65
29 March	Elizabeth wife of William Reynolds	23
	Rev. Thomas Adams (Concord)	<n/g>
10 April	Nancy widow of Thomas Hart	7<unr>
6 April	(N) c/o Jonathan Joseph	5 days
7 April	Mary widow of George H. Atkins	45
4 April	Tilghman Knights (colored), George Moore (colored), & Jack (N) (colored) & 1 more black (N) died near Milton	<n/g>
13 April	Ephraim Kingsberry	60
	Eliza wife of William K. Atkins	25
15 April	Purnal Ennis	60
17 April	Henry Dunning (registrar)	31
	James Bartlett	6
25 April	Susanna Palmore	89
p. 47 ...		
28 April	Mary wife of George R. Fisher	40
3 May	Joseph Maull (governor) – suddenly	<n/g>
13 May	Eli Hall, Sr.	70
17 May	Robert Lolis of Thomas	18
21 May	Elizabeth wife of Jesse Dazey	53

23 May	Elizabeth wife of Jesse Edgin	21
27 May	Cornelia widow of James Davis	56
25 May	Paynter Joseph of Noah	20
26 June	James N. Harris	47
5 July	Anderson Johnson	15 years 20 days
	Mary wife of Greenberry Pepper	25
13 July	(N) c/o James M. Harris	<n/g>
12 July	Manuel Harmon	90
	Margaret J. of William E. Joseph	<n/g>
29 July	(N) c/o William N. Thorogood	16 months
30 July	Andy widow of James Short – suddenly	45
6 September	Mary Ann wife of Capt. J. C. Atkins	25
13 September	Juliana wife of John Bennum	27
14 September	Peter Green – 10 o'clock evening	26
15 August	(N) c/o Benjamin S. Warrington	0 days
2 September	Daniel Rodney	82
23 September	Caroline wife of William Burton	21
25 September	Thomas Salmons, Jr. – consumption	<n/g>
~~24 September~~	~~(N) wife of Edward Honey~~	~~26~~
	Jane Hopkins	60
2 October	~~(N) wife of Joseph Hickman~~	~~25~~
13 October	Mary wife of Francis Rowen	18
	(N) c/o Greensb. Rogers	8 months
10 October	Ellen wife of Dr. James Hudson	<n/g>
15 October	Stephen Warren (C Creek)	65
7 October	Nancy wife of Stephen Blizzard	52

p. 48 ...		
1 November	John Wainright	52
8 or 9 November	Unice Morris – insane	60
19 or 20 November	Mary widow of Phil. Mariner – suddenly	67
25 November	Elizabeth wife of James Walls of E.	50
4 December	Edward Dingle, Esq.	35
3 December	Nancy wife of Samuel Joseph of J.	40
1 December	(N) c/o George Greer (dec'd)	6 months
28 November	one of twins (N) of John W. Moore	5 months
5 December	William H. c/o Bartley Wilson	1
8 December	William A. Cameron (teacher)	70
17 evening or 18 morning December	Christopher Lockrider	50
19 December	(N) c/o John Wise (sheriff)	<n/g>
22 December	a black man (N) shot near Marshyhope, Sussex	<n/g>
September	Stephen Morris	<n/g>
October	Joseph J. Gillis	<n/g>
27 December	Henry Bailey	40
9 December	Brinkley Wilson	50
	1847	
8 January	Ebe Walter	68
11 January	Stephen C. Blizzard	42
19 January	Jane wife of John Robinson	38
16 January	James Miller (Baltimore Hundred)	35

20 January	Richard Jefferson	68
19 January	Charlotte wife of said Richard	60
26 January	Mary widow of Thomas Lolis	62
8 or 9 January	John Aydolett (Baltimore)	42
	John Bunting	<n/g>
	& some 6 or 8 more in Baltimore Hundred	<n/g>
30 January	Elizabeth wife of James Wilson (card.)	30
15 November	George Bennett (C Creek)	30
31 December	John W. Argoe	40
24 December	Nathan Bennet	20
p. 49 ...		
18 December	Sarah wife of Lemuel Draper	45
2 January	Mary widow of Joseph Carey	64
	Nancy wife of William Jefferson	27
7 February	William Smith, Sr.	76
	John Dingle – insane	56
10 February	Rowland s/o John Marvel	16
8 or 9 February	apprentice (N) to James Wilson	12
	(N) c/o said James Wilson	6 months
14 February	Francis Henrietta wife of William H. Swiggett	35
16 February	Ann wife of Lot Rawlins	40
17 February	Absalom Rust	76
	Alexander Draper (Slaughter Neck)	35
15 February	Mary wife of William Watson of Wyn	36
19 February	Nancy widow of John Thorogood, Sr.	57
23 February	John Davidson (Millsboro)	40

26 February	George Culver (Millsboro)	50
	Elizabeth wife of Jacob Crampfield (Millsboro)	42
27 February	(N) d/o Capt. Morris (Millsboro)	15
4 March	Catharine wife of Lemuel Lingo	25
6 March	(N) c/o J. L. Layton	3 weeks
8 March	Elizabeth wife of Jeremiah Kinney	40
last of February	Ezekiel Cooper	84
March	Samuel Brereton	<n/g>
14 March	Joseph Huffington (Concord)	35
4 March	Rachel Pusey at William Thorogood	17
18 March	William Stuart	70
19 March	Robert Frame (lawyer)	47
26 March	John Vaughn (tanner)	47
31 March	John Burbbayge	21
p. 50 ...		
1 April	Samuel F. Conaway	<n/g>
7 April	Margaret Anderson	2
5 April	George Lofland	32
20 April	Hannah of William C. Joseph	5
21 April	Jacob Morris – poor house	55
23 April	William Polk (Milton)	52
25 April	Joshua Short (Dagsboro)	64
27 April	William Thorogood	64
1 May	James Hopkins (Legisl.)	36
26 April	John M. Darby (Milford)	55
7 May	Isaac Roach (near)	35
13 May	John Owens (N.W. Fork)	55

15 May	Sarah d/o William Simpler	10
17 May	Lydia widow of Eli Walls (dec'd)	70
18 May	Catharine wife of Joseph Russel	35
27 May	Avis wife of Peter Prettyman	<n/g>
28 May	& her husband Peter	<n/g>
10 June	Ignatius Taylor (sheriff, Kent)	<n/g>
19 June	Thomas B. s/o Isaac Simpler	13 months
22 June	Sarah widow of Mitchel Scott	45
30 June	(N) of Peter Burton (Rehob.)	<n/g>
7 July	Ezekiel Timmons	70
10 July	Emiline Marsh (Rehob.)	25
	(N) d/o William Goslee (dec'd)	16 months
17 July	Thomas Marsh (Rehob.)	40
23 July	Jessee Edgens	30
5 August	Sarah wife of Thomas W. Hatfield (Georgetown)	25
17 July	Elizabeth wife of Joseph Smith	<unr>
4 August	Enoch Evans (Baltimore)	75
p. 51 ...		
4 August	Elijah Williams	44
	about 60 persons–half men, half women–died in Baltimore Hundred by the first week in August of sore throat or black tongue	<n/g>
25 August	Joshua Burton of Jehu (Long Neck)	25
6 August	Har. Henry M. Ridgely	67
22 August	Riley Wilson (Milton)	58

25 August	Samuel Hurt, Esq.	62
1 September	Capt. Benjamin Potter (Milford)	<n/g>
31 August	(N) c/o John W. Shockley	35 days
13 September	Mary widow of Abraham Reynolds	55
	Elizabeth wife of Elijah Dowel	45
17 September	Jonathan s/o Jon R. Torbert	10 months
20 September	Alexander Warrington	64
23 September	William C. Joseph – found dead; suddenly	51
24 September	John Roach (I. River)	60
28 September	Elizabeth widow of Jessee Darn	80
	(N) widow of John Rust (Seaford)	<n/g>
9 October	Joshua s/o John Spicer	7 months
15 September	Samuel Oliver	54
18 October	Ann widow of Asa Johnson, Sr.	52
20 October	(N) c/o Nelson L. Johnson	8 months
25 October	Sarah Priscilla d/o F. E. Blizzard	14 months
29 October	James Redden of James	25
12 October	Mary Hidaugh Bennum of J.	10 months
11 November	Hugh Linch of James	21
14 November	Jesse Walls of Samuel	32
29 November	Rev. William Spry	35
p. 52 ...		
3 December	Henry C. Waples – 9 a.m.	30
6 December	Lydia Ann wife of George W. Joseph	24

20 December	Sarah wife of Elisha Gothard	23
	Robert Black – brought home 18, from small hurt	52
24 December	John Bennum	32
25 December	Margaret wife of John S. Simpler	25
	1848	
11 January	Capt. Abram Kimmey – died on water	37
25 December	John Willey	<n/g>
11 January	Mary wife of John Jones (Milton)	35
20 January	Burton Prettyman, Sr.	70
	(N) c/o Thomas Palmore	6 months
29 January	Mary widow of William Dean	52
21 January	John S. Simpler	35
31 January	John Wingate (blacksmith)	59
1 February	William Warrington of Ann	23
3 February	Jones Ellinsworth (C Creek)	70
7 February	Jesse Simpler	32
4 February	(N) c/o Leven Mgee	3 weeks
12 February	Catharine wife of Robert Long	30
17-18 February	Rev. Garrett Layton	35
15 February	Prettyman Day	76
19 February	(N) c/o Absal. Dodd, Jr.	<n/g>
15 January	William Marvel	85
3 March	Sarah widow of Luke Lamb	40
	Lydia widow of David Hazzard (Angola)	70
23 February	John Q. Adams	81
16 March	Mary Gordon (Georgetown)	78

24 March	Peter Walls, Sr.	75
	~~Luke Watson (Baltimore Hundred)~~	~~<n/g>~~
p. 53 ...		
14 January	Luke Jacobs	72
23 March	Elizabeth wife of Paynter Watson (Baltimore Hundred)	30
25 March	Mary wife of Capt. Gray (Baltimore Hundred)	30
28 March	Jonathan Jacobs (Baltimore Hundred)	50
31 March	(N) wife of Handy Hastings (Baltimore Hundred)	27
	(N) c/o (N) Wharton (Baltimore Hundred)	<n/g>
28 March	~~Charles Brown (Negro)~~	<n/g>
29 March	John Jacob Aster	<n/g>
9 April	Levicy widow of William Wilson (Prime Hook)	70
12 April	Loadiwick Warren	70
15 April	William Wilson	57
19 April	Absalom Dodd – drowned, 6 o'clock p.m.	6
2 May	Hester widow of Selby Lawson	58
4 May	Warren Jefferson – self shot	60
	William Wilson – suddenly	35
10 May	Zachariah Tam – in 10 hours	60
July	twin Thomas & William c/o Susan Fowler	5 or 6 days
7 July	Laurana widow of James PettyJohn	45
	(N) c/o Rev. J. Morrell	10 months

9 July	Ebe Dutton – 9 o'clock a.m.	30
15 July	Eleanor wife of Robert Lacey	47
	Tabitha wife of Barclay Wilson	44
	(N) wife of Jonathan Williams in childbed of 3 children	<n/g>
	Jonathan Jenkins (First Dover Bank)	<n/g>
14 July	James Bayard, Jr.	24
20 July	Francis Shurck (governor of PA)	70
9 August	Wrixham McIlvaine	63
12 August	John T. Burton	56
p. 54 ...		
12 August	John R. Draper	4
2 September	William B. Ewing (surveyor)	3
26 July	Janette widow of Robert Frame	40
10 September	Coclus Hall (Milsboro)	22
13 September	Ebenezer PettyJohn	91
15 September	Capt. Robert Pointer – died in North Carolina	32
22 September	Jane wife of Benjamin S. Warrington	30
16 September	Henry C. s/o N. W. Walls	<n/g>
20 September	(N) c/o William Powders	1
	Sarah Blizzard	35 years 5 months
28 September	Susanna widow of Eb. PettyJohn	64
29 September	(N) wife of (N) Paipe (Milton, shoemaker)	<n/g>
17 or 24 September	John Prettyman	60
27 October	Mary wife of Jonathan Collins	30

28 October	Sarah wife of Cornelius Coulter	60
30 October	Alfred s/o George H. Atkins	14
23 October	Elisha Dickerson (Carey roads)	50
7 November	Robert Parsons	3
10 November	Theophilus Spicer	50
11 November	Lydia Goslee – 9 o'clock p.m.	21
	Caldwell Marvel	35
15 November	Silas R. c/o Truitt PettyJohn	7 months
30 November	William E. Harris of Benton (Seaford)	40
6 December	Curtis Steen, Jr.	35
	Tamsey wife of William Palmore of Richard (Coolspring)	25
	(N) c/o Joseph R. Layton (Milsboro)	<n/g>
18 December	Elizabeth mother of Jos. Kollock	<n/g>
	William Read, Sr.	<n/g>
	1849	
10 January	Fowler Dodd	65
p. 55 ...		
10 January	Mary Ann Donovan	18
3 February	William Chase, Sr.	60
2 February	(N) Davis sister of William O. Redden (Georgetown) & wife of George R. Davis	<n/g>
4 February	Theodore PettyJohn	24
6 or 7 February	Alcey widow of (N) Smith	75
7 February	Thomas PettyJohn	21
	John Spicer of C.	49
8 or 9 February	Levi Warrington of Luke	24
9 February	William s/o James Butler	8

4 February	Hannah wife of William S. McIlvain	25
15 February	Lydia widow of Thomas Burton	75
16 February	Joseph Shirman	40
23 January	(N) c/o Hannah McBride	<n/g>
25 January	Hannah wife of Robert Arthurs	26
18 February	George Collins – Zachariah Wilson son-in-law	26
28 February	Mary Ann wife of Thomas Franklin	23
1 March	Elijah Melson at L. Blizzard	23
10 March	William Reed, Jr. – suddenly	20
12 or 13 March	Abel Dutten	54
11 March	(N) c/o Lemuel Davidson	34 days
12 March	Frances wife of William Russel, Esq. – midnight	60
	Mary wife of William Pepper	35
	(N) wife of Eli Donavon	<n/g>
	Nancy wife of Robert Hall, Jr.	48
25 March	Joshua S. Layton, Esq.	45
3 April	Elizabeth wife of Pipkin Minor at Baltimore	50
	(N) wife of John D. Marshal (Lewes)	36
13 April	Erasmus Hazzard of Judge	24
20 April	Thomas Simpler, Sr. – 10 o'clock	7
	(N) wife of Charles Vaughn	40
25 April	John Wallace (Milford)	82
p. 56 ...		
27 April	William B. Cooker (ex-governor) – suddenly	78
25 April	Nancy widow of Eli Hall (Milton)	60

6 May	Brinkley L. Walls	36
16 June	Robert Burton (farmer)	77
11 June	James K. Polk (ex-president) – cholera	54
19 June	Maria wife of Robert Houston Proth	4
1 or 3 July	Penelope widow of (N) Walton, Esq.	45
9 July	Edward Harris s/o J. H.H.	18
12 July	John Simpler of Z. – on the road	30
15 July	Edward Willey – in 10 hours	2
19 July	Eber Torbert – in 10 hours	57
24 July	Zipporah wife of Abram Marvel – 3 or 4 weeks sick	40
26 July	John Warrington of John	3
	(N) d/o Eber Torbert	18
28 July	Elizabeth wife of William N. Thorogood	2
	Hetty wife of Eber Torbert	46
31 July	Boaz Warren	65
15 August	Nathaniel Torbert (Mill W.)	35
19 August	Nancy wife of Elisha Carey	40
29 August	Arcada Heartt – slowly	<n/g>
	(N) c/o Isaac Heart	16
27 August	Jesse Griffith & his brother	40
	Manlove Griffith	38
	William Carlisle & mother (N) of William Carlisle 5 days after	<n/g>
19 September	Leven Palmore	40
	George W. B. Johnson (Lerne)	16
	Mary d/o Samuel Palmore	1
6 or 7 September	Isaac Bartlett	45

14 September	Mary widow of Ezekiel Green	69 or 70
4 October	Lemuel Watson	<n/g>
10 October	Thomas McIlvaine (Kent)	62
1 November	Ebenezer C. Joseph (Louth) – fever	23
29 October	(N) – burnt at alms house	<n/g>
22 October	Anlsey White – alms house	70

Index

Job 8
Bartlett
(N) 25
Hester 20
Isaac 25, 58
James 12, 20, 34, 46
Mary 12, 34
Sarah 25
Barton
Joshua 38
Batson
Kendal 26
Bayard
James 55
Bayliss
Elizabeth 12
James F. 12
Beachamp
William 44
Beauchamp
Lenna 15
William 15
Bell
Ann 38
George 32, 38
Ben
Elizabeth 44
Josiah 44
Benky
Jane 33
Bennet
Joshua 41
Nathan 49
Bennett
Caleb P. 23
George 38, 49
Hester 42, 43
John 43
Mary 38
Nehemiah 42
Bennum
George 27
H. O. 37
Hester 41
Hetty 44
J. 52
John 47, 53
Joseph 2
Juliana 47
Mary Hidaugh 52
R. S. 44
Rachel 37
Robert S. 41
Zach 41
Benson
Frances 13
George 42
Henry 13
Mary 21
William 21, 27
Bernard
Derick 16
Bevans
(N) 10
Finley 10
Tindley 3
Biston
Elizabeth 31
Myers 31
Black
James R. 29
Robert 53
Blizzard
(N) 25

Elizabeth 5
F. E. 52
Hester 21
John 23
John H. 22
Kezia 21
L. 57
Levin 22, 25
Margaret 13
Mary 6
Nancy 47
Nathaniel 10
Rachel 45
S. E. 13
Sarah 55
Sarah Priscilla 52
Stephen 21, 47
Stephen C. 48
Thomas 9, 45
William 5
William B. 21

Blocksom
David 8

Bloxom
(N) 37
Richard 37

Bloxum
Richard 14

Blue
Joel 2
Mary 2

Bowlin
Leuranah 40

Boyar
Donovan 14

Bradley
Isaac 36

Brereton
Daniel 45
Patience 37
Samuel 37, 50

Brerton
Myers 27

Brinkloe
John 35

Brittenham
Elizabeth 42

Brown
Charles 54
Elizabeth 2, 39
James 2
John 39
Joseph 39

Buckle
John 24
Joseph 24

Bunnum
Nancy 34
Zachariah 34

Bunting
John 49

Burbbayge
Elizabeth 45
John 30, 45, 50
Rachel 33
Thomas 40

Burrows
John 32

Burton
(N) 11, 23, 36, 43, 51
Adaline 21
Adam 40, 45
Benjamin 7, 14, 21, 39
Bersheba 11

Caroline 47
Coard 34
Coroll 17
D. 36
Daniel 35, 36
Edward 34
Eli. 7
Eliza Ann 17
Hamilton 14
Isaiah 23
James 24
Jehu 51
John 8, 12, 24
John C. 29
John T. 55
Joshua 8, 51
Katharine 14
Louiza 12
Luke 8
Lydia 57
Nathaniel 43
Patience 8
Pemberton 4
Peter 51
Robert 12, 16, 58
Saby 29
Samuel 5
Sarah 34
Sophia 14
Straton 2
Thomas 8, 57
William 15, 47
William Bag. 40
Woolsey 12, 29, 39

Butcher
Comfort 27
Derick 20
Derickson 26, 27
Isabella 20

Butler
Benjamin 9, 11
Elizabeth 11
James 56
William 56

Cadda
John 9

Cade
Eliza 39
John 37, 39
Jonathan 13

Calhoon
James 11
Leven 44
Rachel 44

Cameron
William A. 48

Campbell
(N) 4
Mary 4

Cannon
Benjamin 29
Isaac 35
Jacob 35
Josiah 36
Levi 27
Martha 6
William D. 30

Carey
Anna 3
Eli 3, 30
Elisha 43, 58
Hester 43
John 14

Joseph 11, 18, 49
Mary 49
Nancy 58
Robert 9
Samuel H. 1
Susan 18
Thomas 3, 18
Carlisle
(N) 43, 58
William 58
Carpenter
James 2
Samuel 13
Thomas Wilson 4
Cathell
Gincey 12
Mitchell 12
Cellonis
Bevan 42
Eliza 42
Chase
Eve 18
John 5
Mary 9
William 18, 56
Christopher
Sally 33
Cirwithen
Caleb 42
Clark
Comfort 33
William 1, 33
Clifton
Isaiah 7
Isaih 3
Patience 3
Coalter
Ruth 18
Coffen
Mary 10
Newbould 10
William 39
Coffin
(N) 6
Jordan 25
Kendal S. 15
Newbould 2, 8
Samuel 8
Thomas 6
William 25
William J. 20
Cohoon
(N) 14
Elisha 1
James 29
Josiah 9
Levin 14
Nancy 29
Peter 29
Phoebe 14
Coleman
Thomas 6
Collins
(N) 39
George 57
Horatio 19
John 3, 18
Jonathan 55
Mary 55
Thomas 5
Conaway
Asa 7, 16
Elizabeth 7
Levin 9, 29

Lodowick 2
Mary 29
Samuel F. 50
Connelly
Jane 20
Sophia Ann 32
William 40
William M. 20
Conner
John 23
Lettee 23
Conwell
(N) 31
John 27, 29, 31
William 31
Cooker
William B. 57
Cooper
Ezekiel 50
Thomas 7
Cord
Jane 41
Coulter
Cornelius 56
Elizabeth 4
Sarah 56
Craig
(N) 8
David 8, 18
John 26
Nancy 8
Crampfield
Elizabeth 50
Jacob 50
Cullen
(N) 10
Charles M. 4
Elisha D. 10
Jonathan 5
Culver
George 50

Darby
John M. 50
Darn
Elizabeth 52
Jessee 52
David
John C. 38
Davidson
(N) 57
Janille 12
John 5, 12, 26, 34, 49
Lemuel 57
Richard C. 9
Sarah 34
Davis
(N) 56
Cornelia 47
George R. 56
James 47
John C. 35
Lydia 22
Mark 28, 36
Mary 24
Nelea 24
Samuel 22
Sarah Ann 22
Day
Prettyman 53
Dazey
Elizabeth 46
Jesse 46
Dean

Edmund 31
Jessee 4
John W. 36
Mary 53
William 13, 53
Dennis
Isaac 22
Derickson
Dag 41
Dagworthy 41
Derrickson
Dag 37
Louiza 37
Dewasle
(N) 31
Dickerson
Caroline 8
Edmond 13
Elisha 56
Peter 8
Sarah 13
Somerset 40
Dickeson
Charles 6
Levin 13
Dickinson
Samuel 4
Dickison
Jonathan 6
Dingle
Edward 48
John 49
Dodd
(N) 45, 53
Absal. 53
Absalom 54
Angelia (Hannah) 2
Aora 22
Asahel 20
Cornelia 20
Fowler 56
Hannah 35
John 14
Joseph 14
Mariam 33
Peter 45
Solomon 8
Donavan
(N) 43
Phil. 42
Sarah 42
Wingate 43
Donavon
(N) 57
Eli 57
Donovan
Burton 22
Jacob 11
Kendal 38
Mary Ann 56
Tabitha 38
Dorey
Benjamin 45
Dorman
John 30
Nehemiah 42
Sarah 42
Dowel
Elijah 52
Elizabeth 52
Draper
(N) 41
Alexander 49
John R. 55

Joseph 17
Lemuel 49
Mary 41
Sarah 49
Thomas 41

Drisco
(N) 24

Dukes
Tamar 21

Dunning
Henry 46

Duskey
(N) 24

Dutten
(N) 24
Abel 57
James S. 42
John 11, 14, 15
Richard 24
Richard A. 1
Sarah 15
Thomas 15

Dutton
Ebe 55
Josiah 23
Nol. 15
Penelope 23
Unice 15

Edgens
Jessee 51

Edgin
Elizabeth 47
Jesse 47

Elligood
(N) 14
John 14

Ellinsworth
Jones 53

Elliot
(N) 42
Meshach 42

Ellis
Rhoda 3

Ennis
Adaline 32
Hall 12
John 38
Poel 38
Purnal 32, 46
Samuel 12
Sophia 1
William 1
William B. 2

Evans
Enoch 51
John R. 30
Joseph 32
Nancy 19
Robert 17
Samuel 19

Ewing
Brinkley 5
Gust. A. 45
William B. 55

Fannell
Ann 1

Fausky
John 32

Finall
John 22
Nancy 22
Purnall 22

Findal
(N) 10
Samuel 10
Fisher
Charles 36, 45
Curtis 5
George R. 46
Henry P. 15
Mary 45, 46
Fisk
Wilbur 28
Fleetwood
Mary 28
Flowers
Diademia 41
Samuel 41, 42
Fossett
Ann J. 39
Jacob 39
Foster
Thomas 27
Fowler
Kendal 10
Susan 54
Thomas 54
William 54
Frame
(N) 28
George 28, 44
Janette 55
Robert 50, 55
Francklin
Benjamin 15
Franklin
Mary Ann 57
Thomas 57
Freeman
William 26
Futcher
William 24

Gerard
Stephen 13
Gillis
Joseph J. 48
Godwin
Joseph 2, 16
Levin 10
Nancy 2
Gordon
Elizabeth 1
Mary 53
William 1
Gordy
(N) 25
Aaron 25
Goslee
(N) 37, 51
Elizabeth 11
Job 13, 15
Lettee 37
Lydia 56
Nancy 15
Peter 11, 26
William 17, 26, 37, 45, 51
Gothard
Elisha 53
Sarah 53
Gray
Capt. 54
Mary 54
William 22
Green

Albert 13
Ezekiel 59
Mary 59
Peter 47

Greer
(N) 48
George 48

Grice
Jane 28
Thomas 13, 28, 35
William 13

Griffith
Isaac F. 27
Jesse 58
Manlove 58

Gurley
Nelly 9

Hall
(N) 15
Anna 19
Coclus 55
Edward 19
Eli 46, 57
George 45
Isaac 17
James 1
Maria Catharine 45
Mary 17
Nancy 57
P. 7
Peter 20
Purnall 15
Robert 57
Sally 20
William 7
Woolsey 20, 44

Hamilton
Mary 19
Purnal 19

Handy
J. Backer 20

Hanson
Minah 18
Robert 18

Hardy
John 5
Prudence 5

Harman
(N) 37
Bowen 37

Harmon
Edward 18
Manuel 47
Nathan 41

Harper
John 19
Nancy 19

Harris
(N) 47
Ann 28
Benton 9, 56
Dixon 20
Edward 58
J. H. 21, 58
James A. 28
James M. 47
James N. 47
Margaret 23
Nancy 24
Peter 44
Robert L. 37
Sarah A. 21
William 12, 24

William E. 56
William J. 22, 23
Harrison
W. H. 31
Hart
Nancy 46
Thomas 46
Hartt
Zadock 28
Hastings
(N) 54
Handy 54
Hatfield
Sarah 51
Thomas W. 51
Hays
John 41
Mary 41
Hazzard
Alias 31
Coard 11
D. 39
David 34, 53
Elizabeth 8, 31
Erasmus 57
James 6
Joseph 8
Judge 57
Lydia 53
Selick 3
William S. 27
Heaitt
Zechariah 4
Hearn
George 45
Heart
(N) 58
Isaac 58
Heartt
Arcada 58
Heath
Thomas 24
Hester
Lydia 38
Wallace 38
Hickman
(N) 47
Joseph 47
Mary 9
William 9
Hill
Eliza 7
John 7
Joshua 9
Levi 9, 16, 27
Nehemiah 6
Sarah 16
Stephen 25
Hobbs
George 27
Thomas 21
William 11
Holland
(N) 4
Albert 43
Benjamin L. 5
Elisha 15
Elizabeth Ann 15
Isaac 4, 12
James 18
John 12, 25
Joseph 6
Holstein
Elisha 16

Howard 16
Mary 16
Sally 16
William 1
Honey
(N) 47
Edward 47
Hood
John 26
Hopkins
David 40
Heensy 23
James 50
Jane 47
John 29
Josiah 19
Levi 26
Peter 17
Sophia 40
Houston
Joseph 43
Shepherd 20
Susanna 20
Howell
William 39
Hudson
Elijah 31
Elizabeth 12
Ellen 47
James 38, 47
Mary 35
Theodore 27
Wharris 12
Huffington
Joseph 50
Hunter
Gideon 31
Robert 22
Hurdle
Belinda 34
Jacob 34
Lettee 21
Hurt
Samuel 52

Ingraim
John 14
Mary 14
Ingram
Joshua 29

Jackson
Andrew 44
Andrew C. 9
Jacobs
Jonathan 54
Luke 54
William 22
James
Zadoc 2
Jefferson
(N) 36
Charlotte 49
Jacob 5
Job 27
Katharine 12
Kittury 38
Martha Ann 25
Mary 8
Nancy 49
Richard 49
Robert 36
Warren 21, 54
William 8, 12, 21, 27,

36, 49
Jenkins
Jonathan 55
Jester
Daniel 19, 29
Isaac 19
John Smith 21
Johnson
(N) 5, 25, 28, 31, 34, 52
Abram 2
Anderson 7, 10, 47
Ann 52
Annanias 43
Asa 30, 52
Azel 25
Benjamin 45
Brinkley 32
Brinkly 23
Burton 5, 11
Caleb 23
Elizabeth 19, 28, 40
George W. B. 58
Hannah W. 28
Henrietta Jane 23
James 29, 40
James C. 19
Jesse 1
Joshua 30
Lemuel 3
Louisa 7
Love 4
Lovey 28
Mary 12, 16
Mills 6
Nancy 31, 32
Nath. M. 31
Nelson 23, 25, 28, 34
Nelson L. 40, 52
Perry 19
Peter 3
Purnal 40, 43
Richard 3, 16, 28
Robert 25, 31
Robert L. 31
Robert McFerrin 33
S. W. 28
Samuel 16, 19
Samuel P. 3
Sarah 4
Silas 12
Slater 4
Staten 11
W. W. 5
William 4, 40
Jones
(N) 42
Isaac 32
John 53
Louder 10
Mary 53
Nathaniel 10
Philip 42
Thomas A. 42
William 32
Zipporah 42
Joseph
(N) 7, 30, 31, 44, 46
Amy 45
Ann M. 3
Asbury 30
Bayard 44
Belinda 10
Burton 30, 33

Ebenezer 45
Ebenezer C. 59
Elihu 37
Elisha 3
Elizabeth 1, 32
Elon 3
Ephraim 1
George W. 31, 52
Gideon 23
Hannah 50
Harriett 7
Hezekiah 15, 19
J. 26, 48
James B. 30
Jonathan 10, 20, 46
Lydia Ann 52
Margaret J. 47
Mary 17, 25
Mary Ann 43
Nancy 33, 48
Nathan 10
Noah 7, 24, 30, 43, 47
Patience 26
Paynter 3, 7, 47
Samuel 1, 26, 32, 48
Sarah 24
Sarah Ann 28
Theodore W. 19
Thomas 19, 32
William 23
William C. 45, 50, 52
William E. 47
William S. 28
Winny 1
Zechariah 25, 34

Justis
Martha 6

Justus
(N) 22
Martha 22

Kendrick
(N) 35
William 35

Kimmey
(N) 40
Abram 53
Jacob 40

King
(N) 22
Charles 22
William 22

Kingsberry
Ephraim 46

Kinney
Elizabeth 50
Jeremiah 50

Knights
Tilghman 46

Kollock
Adaline 40
Ann 11
Elizabeth 20, 56
George 11
John 40
Jos. 56
Myra 46
Philip 20

Lacey
Eleanor 55
Elizabeth 2
Hezekiah 17
Rhoda 17

Robert 2, 17, 55
Spencer 2
Lamb
Luke 20, 53
Sarah 53
Lank
(N) 28
Leven 12, 13
Mitchell 28
Susanna 13
Thomas 26
William 18, 20
Lawles
John 39
Nancy 18
Stephen 18
Lawlis
John 40
Lawson
(N) 3, 4
Hannah 7
Henry 3, 4
Hester 54
James 6, 39
Jehu 16
Mary 39
Nathaniel 4
Selby 7, 23, 54
Thomas 7
Layton
(N) 50, 56
Garrett 53
J. L. 50
J. S. 39
Joseph R. 56
Joshua S. 57
Louder 36
Sarah Ann 39
Lewis
Metilda 2
Wrixham 16
Linch
Hugh 52
James 52
Jeremiah 12
John 24
Joseph 37
Lingo
(N) 18
Alice 3
Burton 33
Catharine 50
Elisha 29
Eliza 29
Henry 3, 10, 15, 26, 31, 38
Jesse 30
John 3, 18, 30
John Robinson 17
Lemuel 50
Lydia 31
Nancy 8, 15
Samuel 8, 19
Lockrider
Christopher 48
Lockwood
Samuel 13
Lofland
George 50
Isaac 21
James P. 42
Nehemiah 32
Nutter 19
Lolis

Mary 49
Robert 46
Thomas 46, 49
Long
Catharine 53
Robert 53
Lybrand
Joseph 39
Lyons
(N) 33
L. L. 33

Mace
B. L. 40
Maclin
Mary Anne 29
Mails
Joseph 32
Males
Joseph 23
May 23
Marine
(N) 41
Ann C. 41
Robert 41
Mariner
Comfort 2
Mary 48
Phil. 48
Robert 2
Marsh
Emiline 51
Joseph 15
Thomas 51
Marshal
(N) 57
John D. 57
Martin
(N) 6
John 7
Josiah 35
Samuel 6
Marvel
(N) 31
Aaron 23
Abram 58
Adam 9
Caldwell 56
David 34
Deborah 14
Ed. 39
Eleanor 29
Elizabeth 3
George 14, 21
John 33, 45, 49
Joseph 31
Kendal 32
Lydia 33
Mary 21
Rowland 49
Sarah A. 42
Theodore 42
Thomas 23
William 53
Zipporah 58
Marvil
David 1
John P. 7
Mary 11
Sarah Townsend 7
Mase
Jacob 33
Massey
(N) 15

John 15
Maull
(N) 28
G. W. 28
Joseph 46
Miss (N) 27
Nehemiah 6
Mcally
(N) 20
McBride
(N) 57
Hannah 57
McCabe
(N) 17
Garrettson 17
McFerran
Robert 36
Mcgee
William 26
McIlvain
Hannah 57
William S. 57
McIlvaine
(N) 14, 43
B. 35
Benjamin 24, 43, 45
David 6
Jane 45
Jane Benky 33
John 14
Tabitha 24
Thomas 59
William 2
Wrixham 55
Meloney
Isaac 43
Melson
Elijah 57
Meria
Austin 13
Henrietta 13
Meriner
Mary 28
Philip W. 28
Messeck
George 39
Jonathan 36
Sarah 36
Messick
(N) 21
Coventon 21
George 45
Isaac 15
John 3
Mgee
(N) 53
Leven 53
Mary 23
William 23
Middleton
James 2
John 18
Milby
Arthur 43
Mary 38
Zadoc 38
Miller
James 48
Minor
Elizabeth 57
Pipkin 57
Mitchelmore
John 18
Moor

Nancy 9
Moore
(N) 48
David 32
George 46
John W. 48
William 32
Morrell
(N) 54
J. 54
Morris
(N) 50
Burton 21, 44
Capt. 50
Edy 20
Heavilow 45
Isaac 9
Jacob 9, 12, 50
James 42
Jane 34
Jos. 20
Joseph 13
Joshua 33
Lacey 2
Maria 25
Nancy 44
Parker 41
Rachel 6, 12
Robert 16
Stephen 34, 48
Tabitha 2
Thomas 21
Unice 48
William 5
William B. 25
Wingate 6
Zipporah 16
Mumford
John 7, 25
Nicey 7
Mustard
Cornelius 34
David 26
Hester 14
John 14
Margaret 34

Neal
John 41
Joseph 41
Negro
(N) 17, 18, 48
Jack 46
Nelson
Abraham 28

Oliver
Hannah 31
Joseph 31
Samuel 52
Owens
John 50

Paipe
(N) 55
Palmore
(N) 3, 27, 53
Catharine 41
Eleanor 26
Elizabeth 7, 29, 32
Elzey 3, 22, 36
John 26, 27, 29, 42
John P. 21
John W. 44

Jonathan 16
Leven 58
Mary 58
Nathan 6
Prudence 26
Richard 14, 56
Robert Henry 36
Ruth 6
Sally 16
Samuel 58
Sarah 21
Solomon 4
Susanna 46
Tamsey 56
Thomas 53
W. H. 7
William 14, 21, 25, 32, 44, 56
Wools H. 41
Woolsey H. 25

Parker
David 3
George 39, 44
James 43
John 23, 42
Margaret 44
P. 42
Peter 21
Rebecca 21
Samuel 28

Parsons
Hopkins 11
Jane 11
Robert 56
Sally 21
William 15, 21

Passwaters
Jesse 23

Paynter
Alice 19
George 39
John P. 44
Samuel 44

Peckerton
William 33

Pennywell
Elisha 21

Pepper
Burton 2
Chloe 37
Eli 37
George 30
Greenberry 47
Mary 47, 57
Thomas 10
William 57

Perry
James 37
William 37

PettyJohn
(N) 33
Abel 22
E. 42
Eb. 55
Ebenezar 6
Ebenezer 40, 55
James 33, 42, 54
Laurana 54
Mary 6
Silas R. 56
Susanna 55
Theodore 56
Thomas 9, 56
Truitt 56

Zachariah 31
Philips
Chloe 29
Phillips
Spencer 38
Pierce
Mary 43
William 43
Plumber
Robinson 9
Pointer
Robert 55
Polite
Sarah 46
William 20, 46
Polk
George 19
James K. 58
William 50
Pool
Benjamin 17
Gilbert 18
Job 4
John 22
Perry 14, 18, 22
William 18, 20
Potter
Benjamin 52
Powders
(N) 15, 55
Francis 13, 15
Sarah 13
William 55
Prettyman
(N) 6, 16, 43
Ann 31, 36
Avis 51
Burton 4, 53
Eliza 11
Emory 18
George 1, 25, 34
Hester 1
James 43
John 13, 30, 31, 36, 43, 55
Joseph 26
Lany 18
Lydia 4, 43
Mariah 30
Penelope 44
Peter 51
Rachel 6
Robert William 40
Sarah 34
Stephen 25
Warren 16, 44
William 6
Pride
George 10
Woolsey 21
Proth
Maria 58
Robert Houston 58
Pusey
Rachel 50

Quigg
William 4

Rawlins
Ann 49
Lot 49
Read
Abram 26

William 56
Redden
James 52
William O. 56
Reed
Joseph 21
William 57
Reese
Anna 44
William 44
Rench
(N) 10
M. 10
Reynold
Roderick 9
Sarah 9
Reynolds
(N) 13
Abraham 52
Abram 19
Elizabeth 46
Leurana 39
Mary 52
Roderick 13
Thomas 15
William 39, 46
Zechariah 18
Rhodes
William 10
Richards
(N) 16, 37
David 37
Edward 16
Rickards
(N) 37
James 12, 45
Levin 12
Mary 45
Molton 36
William 37
Rider
(N) 44
William 44
Ridgely
Charles G. 40
Har. Henry M. 51
Nicholas 8
Rigely
C. G. 27
Elizabeth 27
Rigware
(N) 38
Mitchell 38
Riley
Elizabeth 44
Gabriel 32
Johnson 8
Thomas 44
Roach
George 16
Isaac 50
James 35
John 52
Nancy 35
Robertson
John 5
Robinson
(N) 28
George 13, 18, 44
James 7
Jane 48
John 48
Parker 35
Peter 13, 23, 28

Gilley 27
James 33, 47
John 21, 39
Joshua 50
Leonard 40
Levi 39
Nancy 27
Philip 21, 38, 42
Purnal 28
Purnall 21
Shurck
Francis 55
Simple
George F. 25
Nancy 26
P. 25
William 26
Simpler
(N) 11, 37
Amos 37
Hester 43
Isaac 51
James 31
Jesse 53
John 58
John S. 53
Leah 1
Margaret 53
Mary 15, 27
Peter 43
Richard 17
Sarah 31, 51
Thomas 1, 15, 57
Thomas B. 51
William 51
Z. 58
Simpson
Leuranah 20
Purnal 20, 21
Sipple
(N) 39
Thomas B. 39
Smith
(N) 34, 56
Alcey 56
David 21
Elizabeth 51
John 21
Joseph 51
Josiah H. 42
Silas 34
William 49
Spearman
Mary 41
Simon 41
Spicer
(N) 24
Alfred R. 24
C. 56
Curtis 15
Eustic James 33
John 16, 45, 52, 56
Joshua 52
Letty 21
Lewis 42
Peter 34
Rhoda 15
Robert 45
Sarah 24
Theodore 14, 21
Theophilus 56
William 24
William B. 27
Spry

William 52
Stan
(N) 25
James 25
Starr
James 24
Steel
(N) 1, 29
Benjamin 2
James 1, 29
Ruth 2
Steen
Curtis 56
Steet
Ann 37
John 37
Stephenson
Maria 46
William 1, 46
Steward
(N) 17
David 17
Stockton
Thomas 46
Stokely
Benjamin 1
Jehu 9, 17
Nancy 1
Patience 26
Sarah 17
Strong
Ashbel 30
Stuart
John 12, 13
Mary 12
William 50
Sullivan
Rachel 11
Swiggett
Francis Henrietta 49
William H. 49

Tam
Joseph 5
Zachariah 54
Taylor
Ignatius 51
Tharp
James 2
Thomas
Abel 25
Thorogood
(N) 47
Elihu 31
Elizabeth 58
John 29, 38, 49
Mary 29
Nancy 49
William 38, 50
William N. 47, 58
Thoroughgood
John 38
Timmons
Ezekiel 51
Tindal
Eliza 31
Eliza Ann 32
James 31, 32
Purnal 15
Toomy
Mary 17
Torbert
(N) 58
Eber 30, 58

Hetty 58
Jon R. 52
Jonathan 52
Lawrence 14
Nancy 14
Nathaniel 58
Peter 30
Robert 10

Truit
David 43
Mary 43

Truitt
George 17
Mary 7

Tull
Sophia 28

Valentine
Jane 34

Vaughan
Leven 41

Vaughn
(N) 57
Charles 3, 57
John 50

Veasey
(N) 43
Lettee 26
Wallace 43
William 26

Veazey
William 11
Zadock 14

Vent
(N) 27
William 27

Vickars
Ed. 29
Edward 43
Mary 29

Virden
Mitchel 26

Wadhams
Benjamin T. 10

Wainright
John 48

Walker
James 16
Mary 16
Nancy 18
Thomas 18

Wall
Elizabeth 42
Gideon 42

Wallace
John 57

Waller
(N) 23
Elizabeth 33
Richard 23
Robert 13, 33

Wallis
Burton 39
Samuel 39
William Henry 39

Walls
(N) 6, 14, 33, 38
Ann M. 32
Arcada 37
Brinkley L. 36, 58
Burton 17
Charles Henry 30
D. L. 33

William 33
Wardle
William 20
Warren
Asa 3, 20, 22
Benjamin 1
Boaz 58
Elizabeth 35
Loadiwick 54
Mary Ann 44
Nancy 22
Priscilla 3, 19
Robert 4, 35, 44
Stephen 47
Warring
Alexander 41
Joseph Alford 41
Warrington
(N) 33, 47
Alexander 36, 52
Ann 53
Anna 23
Benjamin S. 47, 55
Coard 35
Gardiner W. 39
James 11, 46
Jane 55
Jehu 22, 30
John 58
Joseph 7, 10
Joseph H. 22
Levi 56
Luke 56
Lydia 30
Margaret 27
Mary 10, 11
Mary Ellen 37
Polly 17
R. 37
Robert 33, 36, 37
Samuel 16
Sarah 37
Sarah Ann 39
William 53
William C. 35
Watson
Alice 5
Beniah 41
Elizabeth 54
Lemuel 59
Luke 54
Mary 49
Paynter 54
Samuel 27
William 49
Wyn 49
Way
(N) 36
E. J. 36
John 17
Webster
Noah 36
Wells
(N) 25
E. D. 25
Elizabeth D. 11
William H. 6, 11
Welsh
(N) 28
N. D. 28
Wesley
Richard 18
West
(N) 35

Ann 33, 38
Benjamin 37
Elizabeth 30
James 3, 6
John 23, 33, 34, 38
John M. 43
Richard 36
Thomas G. 25, 30
William 37

Wharton
(N) 54
Elisha 9

White
Anlsey 59
Eliza 5
Jacob 5
John 7
Nancy 5
William 5

Willey
Edward 58
John 53

Williams
(N) 19, 55
Elijah 51
Elizabeth 42
John 19
Jonathan 55
Nathan 8
Robert 42

Wills
(N) 18
E. L. 18

Willson
Joseph 29
Patience 2
Richard 2

Wilson
(N) 24-26, 34, 49
Abram 14, 23
Barclay 55
Bartley 48
Brinkley 48
David 10
Ebenezer 12
Elizabeth 38, 49
Elzey 35
Hold 35
Isaac 10, 41
Isabella 13
Jacob 27, 39
James 31, 49
John 9, 35, 40
Jonathan J. 26
Joseph 6, 36
Josh. 40
Joshua 11, 26
Levicy 54
Lewicy 32
Lodawick 3
Margaret 1, 44
Martha 6, 25
Mary 11, 43
Minos 38
Nancy 9, 40
Rachel 23
Reuben 13
Rhodes 40
Richard 25
Riley 39, 51
S. K. 25
S. R. 24, 29
Samuel P. 44
Sarah Jane 41

www.ingramcontent.com/pod-product-compliance
Lightning Source LLC
Chambersburg PA
CBHW072209270326
41930CB00011B/2585
9780806357072